About the book

Even Me is a book about an unworthy feeling young woman who struggled with the scars and brokenness that were caused by a series of life interruptions. Living her life without the father whose love she so desperately craved caused her to look for love in all the wrong places. Becoming a single parent at the age of 20 made her realize that her life was not over, but just beginning. Losing loved ones and the shattering of hopes and dreams made her more dependent upon God.

Even Me is about the inner strength that was found to overcome the many obstacles that were set before her. One day this young woman had a personal encounter with God that led her to being delivered from sinful acts that has kept her in bondage for years and the restoration that brought her to realize how worthy she was.

Even Me is a book that will encourage a single parent, cause a person to believe in the Promises of Jesus, but most importantly, will lead some soul to their deliverance. Be it man, woman, boy or girl; God used me and he can still use you.

After reading *Even Me*, I hope and pray that some young women or young man will realize that not all of life interruptions are meant for bad; but meant for your good.

EVEN ME

Once Scarred and Broken, Now Worthy

Alisha Byrd

AuthorHouse™
1663 Liberty Drive
Bloomington, IN 47403
www.authorhouse.com
Phone: 1-800-839-8640

© 2010 Alisha Byrd. All rights reserved.

No part of this book may be reproduced, stored in a retrieval system, or transmitted by any means without the written permission of the author.

First published by AuthorHouse 9/30/2010

ISBN: 978-1-4520-6243-3 (e)
ISBN: 978-1-4520-6241-9 (sc)
ISBN: 978-1-4520-6242-6 (hc)

Library of Congress Control Number: 2010913417

Printed in the United States of America

This book is printed on acid-free paper.

Because of the dynamic nature of the Internet, any Web addresses or links contained in this book may have changed since publication and may no longer be valid. The views expressed in this work are solely those of the author and do not necessarily reflect the views of the publisher, and the publisher hereby disclaims any responsibility for them.

To the love of my life Chastity
I pray that you are as proud of me as I am of you
I love you more than you will ever know. Besides knowing
God, you are the best thing that ever happened to me

Reviews

The words in this book speak to your heart and touch your soul; hence, enabling me to capture a few sentimental moments in time that's parallel to the life of the author. It is written in Psalm 34:18, "The righteous cry out, and the Lord hears them; He delivers them from all their troubles," it is more than evident that the Lord delivers you from troubles, challenges and even what we perceive to be defeats and this was clearly illustrated in the writing that resides between the front and back cover of this book. Psalm 34:19 denotes, "The Lord is close to the brokenhearted and saves those who are crushed in spirit." Even Me, provides an anecdote that reflects this message and leaves you knowing that there is a God and He can fix whatever you are going through; in the mist He has already worked it out for your good.

Sharon M. Thompson, *Entrepreneur*

I shed tears as I read *Even Me* because I knew of the many challenges Alisha faced from childhood into adulthood. She has written from her heart and is sending a message to all who are scarred and broken. She assures us a relationship with God is the only way to fill every void in our lives. God makes us worthy, when we give him our all.

Elder Katie B. Crockett

Even Me, written by Alisha Byrd whom I love and adore and have found to be a daughter, shows how much she truly loves Christ. 2 Corinthians 3:17 says; Now the Lord is the Spirit, and where the Spirit of the Lord is, there is freedom. In this book, I see that Alisha has received her true freedom from Christ. She has expounded on issues that have happened in her life that some people would rather keep between them and God. In order to receive total restoration, we have to expound on our own issues as well. You will find in life, that if we give our issues to God, there will be total restoration for our souls. My prayer is that whoever reads this book, will receive true deliverance and healing that only comes from God.

God Bless You Alisha, I love you.

Clarissa Wilkerson, Entrepreneur

After reading *Even Me: Once Scarred and Broken, Now Worthy*, I felt inspired. From the very beginning of the book I was gripped by the irony of the author. The author's transparency was a release of all of the anger and pain inside that the she had witnessed or endured during her life. Being transparent is easily seen through or detected and free from guile, candid, obvious. The need to be free from any encompassing demons and albatross in the author's life lends credence to paralleling it to the lives of the reader. I feel this book will enable other readers to relate to the author's trials and struggles and relish in the fact that strength can be pulled from the work to compare to their lives. Starting anew and fresh would be the key for any reader. I highly recommend *Even Me*.

Roger Hyman, MS, LPC
Psychotherapist

I found *Even Me: Once Scarred and Broken, Now Worthy* to be extremely wonderful and I have truly been inspired by the author's transparency. This book made me re-evaluate my strengths and weaknesses as a single-parent. Alisha Byrd allowed God to use her in a way that will touch the lives of many. This book will most definitely be helpful tool to men and women, both young and old.

Apostle S.L. Gillespie

God puts us through test to see how well we can handle situations that he puts before us. Even Me: Once Scarred and Broken, Now Worthy specifies the weakness and strength of a woman overcoming heartache and pain but she is still standing because of God's grace, mercy and peace.

She has become triumphant from past mistakes, been shown and taught to take the paths of the Lord. Even through her life interruptions, you will be inspired to acknowledge God and lean not unto your own understanding and to let his goodness and mercy follow you all the days of your life.

Patricia Byrd- Sturdivant

Contents

The Purpose xiii
Introduction xv

Part One *1*
Once Scarred: Life Interruptions & Obstacles

Life's Interruption One: Getting Pregnant 3
Life Interruption Two: Becoming a Single Parent 7
Life Interruption Three: The death of Uncle John 11
Life Interruption Four: Becoming Unemployed 17
High Hopes 21
Dreams 23
Life Interruption Five The death of Monica 31

Part Two *37*
Once Broken: A Mended Heart

Church Hurt 41
Grace 47
Forgiveness 49
Mercy 53
Deliverance 55
Peace 59
Restoration 61
Favor 65
God's Master Plan 67
An Answered Prayer 71

Part Three *79*

Now Worthy: The Fruits Of The Spirit

Love... 83
Joy.. 85
Patience... 87
Kindness... 89
Goodness... 91
Faithfulness   A Living Sacrifice to God............. 93
Gentleness... 95
Self-Control   Listening and Doing................... 97
Conclusion... 99
Remembering Where I Come From........................ 105

The Purpose

I am a firm believer that everything in life happens for a reason. We complain when we don't get what we think we deserve. We complain once we get it. For years I wanted to know my purpose in life. I have been exposed to some situations and have taken on some duties that only God knew I would be able to handle. However, there are some things that I am still waiting on God to reveal to me.

Being a fatherless child at an early age and struggling with it as an adult has taught me that I am dependent on God and Him only. I have come to the realization that God interrupted my parental bloodline so that he could fulfill my purpose in life.

Becoming a single parent sooner than planned taught me so many lessons. In the process I became determined, educated, independent and strong. God introduced me to those things as a single parent so that my steps as a woman will be ordered by Him and Him only.

Being scarred and broken was God's way of showing me

that only he could make me whole again and worthy of all He has for me. People will hurt you, mistreat, and abuse you. You still have to allow God to use you in spite of the hurt and pain. God used me and he can use you.

Introduction

Reading my Bible and praying is something that I have always been encouraged to do. Yet still there were times when praying was too painful and reading my Bible was just foreign to me. One year I asked my mother for a parallel Bible for Christmas so that I could have gained a better understanding of what I was reading. I would always take detailed notes in church and then go back to review the sermon However, if I needed to refer back to the Bible, I wanted to have the same understanding as other "church folks" seemed to. I started to concentrate on one book in the bible, two scriptures in particular, that I have been self drawn to and called my own.

Proverbs 3: 5-6 (KJV). "Trust in the LORD with all your heart, and lean not on your own understanding; in all your ways acknowledge Him, And He shall direct your paths."

That scripture has become the story of my life to this day, consisting of a series of ups and downs and emotional roller coasters from an early age until now. Growing up without a father whose blood I carry has left a scar that

MAC, Covergirl and Maybelline couldn't cover up and even Mederma, Neosporin and band-aids couldn't heal. This void was so deep that if it was not cleansed with forgiveness, every now and then, it might have destroyed me. Thank God that His timing is different compared to our timing.

As a child, I used to envy how my classmates would talk about the things that their dads had done or made promises to do for them. Those were the days when I wished that I could walk in their shoes and not my own. I wanted my story to be similar to theirs. It was then that I was introduced to a feeling called *emptiness.*

It's amazing how doctors can find remedies and medications for nausea, headaches, colds, and the flu but can't find anything for emptiness.

I've always been puzzled when certain medicines require you to coat your stomach before taking them to eliminate adverse reactions. What happens when you don't have an appetite? Or can't keep food down and are literally running on "empty" but need the medicine? It's sad to say, that I carried this feeling of emptiness around with me for 33 years. Knowing there's a better way, medicine for my soul but not able to coat my stomach so I could digest the medicine my God had prescribed.

Travel with me down memory lane for just a few minutes. It was in college when I thought that I had found "the one." The sweet stories were so on point that skipping class was a norm. Listening to those sweet stories and abandoning what I knew was right led me to become a single parent at age 20.

There I was a junior in college and I had to make a decision that would cause me to slow down or speed up.

About four years ago I was given a CD by a woman at church; she told me "this is exactly what you need to hear." The CD was "Elect Lady" by Bishop Eddie Long. I thought what is an "Elect Lady" and why would she consider me one? First, I looked at her crazy because first of all, why would she give me, of all people this CD? What words could Bishop Eddie Long say that would pertain to me? So much so that she thought I needed to hear it.

Later that night I went home, put my headphones on, transitioned into a receptive mode and listened to a sermon that would ultimately come to change my life. The words flowed from Bishop Eddie Long's mouth as if he was standing right in front of me. He spoke about life's interruptions, why God had elected you to do things that other people can't handle. But most importantly, he spoke about grace, mercy, peace and favor.

The words were so profound, powerful and on point that I could not wait to share the CD with my mother. After she listened to it, we found ourselves constantly in battle over the CD, and sometimes slipping it away from one another. Both of us heard things that pertained to our lives as women and mothers. Bishop Eddie Long stated "that until you accept what God has called you to do, you will never have a day of peace;" I decided after I listened to it 7 times, I must tell my story.

Part One

Once Scarred:
Life Interruptions & Obstacles

"Never let someone use you head for a hat rack,", was something that my Uncle John would always tell me. There are some people who are going to envy the education and status that you will obtain, but remain confident in "who "you are and "whose" you are.

Life's Interruption One: Getting Pregnant

*It's amazing how quickly "bad" news spreads,
like being in college and getting pregnant.*

When I went off to college, I prayed about the direction that God would take me. The only thing he revealed to me was becoming a doctor. So right off top I knew my major had to be Biology. It had been spoken and I had received just that. I didn't give much thought about what kind of doctor I would be; but I knew I was going to be one. I didn't care too much for dealing with sick people; but surely that would eventually grow on me, Right?

I arrived at Winston Salem State University, the summer of August 1994, found my way around campus and registered for classes. I made it through the first semester just fine, making the Dean's List. In my mind, I was well on my way.

During the second semester, I took a Chemistry class and one called Greek and Latin Roots wasn't sure why I needed that to become a doctor. I was headed straight for academic probation because of those classes. You know how it is when you know, that you know, that you know, that something is not for you....this was one of those times. I called myself finding "other "classes to take in their place until I was ready to handle them. Here comes a voice, "This is not the time for failure." Not the time for what? Was all that I could ask. I went back to my room, looked through the course catalog and found another major. I ended up changing to Political Science thinking this would be a good path to get to Law School. This time around, I enjoyed all of my classes, even the ones that I skipped because I was sneaking off to Appalachian State to visit my then boyfriend and thinking I was grown. I ended up double majoring in Political Science and History. At this point my mind was made up-- Law School here I come. But I hadn't consulted God about what I needed to do; or what His will was.

"Pardon the interruption # 1". I got pregnant right after declaring my second major. How would I explain to my mom and grandmother that I was at college having too much fun? Somewhere between acceptance and confusion, my grandmother gave me the option to stay at home and raise my child or to stay in Winston Salem and come home on the weekend after she was born. Ok, I thought, "I'll cross that bridge once I get there."

It's amazing how quickly "bad" news spreads, like being

in college and getting pregnant. I hadn't talked to my dad in years, but the word sure spread to him in Atlanta. He called and said some words that awakened that felling called emptiness, "If I had been there this would have never happened". My thoughts were "where are you now? I'm pregnant and you still aren't here." However; he made it his business to call at least three times a week during my pregnancy to see how things were going. In my opinion, it was cool because I thought that my baby was going to change things and make him come back home. Wrong! He was still away and the emptiness was still there.

Months later, I gave birth to a beautiful baby girl who is now a beautiful young woman. She's fourteen and I am clueless as ever of how to tell her about a man that I barely know, one that she met once in her life and could very well not see again.

One of the many things that I am thankful to God for is the fact that He was considerate enough to guard the heart of my daughter. He placed a father in her life who has always been active, supportive, cheers her on throughout life, takes his role and name of "father" seriously.

Life Interruption Two: Becoming a Single Parent

Alisha Byrd

> *"I knew I had to pick myself up and keep on going. Not knowing where I was headed but I kept going. "*

I commuted to school for a year and a half. My classes were scheduled on Tuesdays and Thursdays and took anywhere from 15 to 18 hours a semester so that I could graduate on time. My daughter's father decided that he didn't want to be in a relationship with me at the time. My baby was one year old and I was raising her while he was 150 miles away, which means I'm on my own. You know how we do when things are going wrong, we turn to God. I had been saved and accepted God in my life, but I've never had the relationship were I sat at his feet and talked to him. I knew I had to pick myself up and keep on going. I didn't know where I was headed, but I kept going.

I graduated within 4 ½ years like I was supposed to. My family and close friends were there to cheer me on; with one person missing—my dad. I could see how proud my family and friends were and that meant a lot; but I wanted my dad. He had missed out on my junior and senior proms, high school graduation, and the birth of my daughter. And being the first to graduate in my family was major to me and something that I wanted him to be proud of.

Five years later, my father's father died. At this time, I was working at a local non-profit as the Office Manager. Some family members asked for my help in locating my dad. They had a general idea of where he lived but no address. I contacted some of the homeless shelters in Atlanta and found him. He came home for the funeral and met my daughter who was five for the first time. We talked, laughed and cried. It didn't feel like he had been gone for as long as he had. It was like I had just talked to him the day before, even though thirteen years had passed since I'd seen him. He said "that even though he had not been there, he was proud of the woman that I had become and vowed to remain in our lives this time." I wasn't buying it but I was willing to give him a second chance.

I later took a job working with the individuals with special needs. I had a Bachelor's degree and had been working for 2 years; but still wasn't making very much. At that point, I had a descent prayer life. So I consulted God as to why I was there, making little of nothing and not moving up in my career. He informed me that the people that He called me to be around had no cares in the world. Some of them may not know what day of the week it is but are satisfied with who they are and what they have. They can come to a place where money and status doesn't matter. I was reminded not get caught up in what I didn't have but to position myself to receive what He has for me.

Life Interruption Three: The death of Uncle John

"All I want to know is "why was I chosen" to watch an uncle that I love so dearly go through something like this."

My grandmother's brother, which was my Uncle John, contacts me stating that he needs my help. I was thinking that he needed a ride somewhere or some pocket change to get him over the hump. It was a lot more serious than that. In finding out about his need caused me to question God once again.

Uncle John had been diagnosed with lung cancer and needed someone to care for him and someone he could trust to manage his finances. Uncle John had been in a mental institution and before the Social Security Administration and Veterans Affairs would release money for his care, there had to be proof that someone would manage his finances and keep a ledger indicating how every penny was spent. After receiving confirmation from God, my full-time job became a part-time job with added on obligations. I immediately became his guardian and custodian without fully understanding what becoming those things meant. I did not know that the responsibility included a small stipend for taking care of him and providing him with transportation. Talking about grace, when I didn't deserve it God showed, EVEN ME grace and favor He'd put in place.

Here I was handling my grandparents and Uncle John's finances, plus juggling the duties of being a single parent with a part-time income. As the months went on, I found myself in the oncologist office with my uncle more than Marshalls and Ross, two of my favorite retail therapies. I wanted to know "why was I chosen to watch an uncle that I loved so dearly, go through something like this." He has two children both living, plenty of nieces and nephews; but God still wanted me to take care of him.

I consulted God about what was next, He informed me that I needed to go back to school. Yeah right; I struggled to obtain the degree that I have. I still wasn't working in my field and my load was heavier than ever. One day, seemingly out of the blue, a commercial came on about a graduate program and the slogan "We Fit Your Life" was ironic. At that time, my life consisted of so much, I wasn't sure I could make it work. Weeks went by and I saw the commercial again; this time I called to get information about the programs offered. Still unsure about why I should go back to school; I consulted

God again while listening to some on hold music, waiting for a representative to come on the line. During our conversation, the commercial came on again. I wanted to shout, "I'm on hold with the school now, shucks, stop showing the commercial."

I had been working closely with the HR Manager on my part-time and had developed an interest in that role logically. Therefore, I enrolled in the MBA program and selected Human Resource Management as my concentration. This was a two year program but I was told that I could finish earlier if I went to every session they offered. I thought, "two years are you serious?" That seemed way too long from the standing line. Once again, God's grace reigned in my life and I ended up finishing six months ahead of time.

Unfortunately, at my next graduation, I had two sets of empty feelings, Uncle John, a man that I had become so close to had lost his battle with cancer and my dad still wasn't there. Foolishly, I went back to God and questioned why he would bring another man into my life only to take him away from me like that. Don't get me wrong, I knew my uncle had lung cancer had lived a long life. It's just that the relationship that Uncle John and I developed was one of co-dependency. I needed to be needed as much as he needed me. It seemed like as soon as we became close, God took him away. While I have a relationship with my maternal grandfather, the bond with Uncle John was different and so much more involved.

I had to pull myself together, and plan funeral arrangements for a man that had added so much to my life. He always told me to *"Never let someone use your head for a hat rack."* But what did that really mean? What in the world is he talking about? It wasn't until God gave me additional mercy and peace that I fully understood it. He poured so much into me in such a short time that even though he's passed his wisdom has been properly invested in me.

Months passed and I found myself with extra time on my hands and very little money in my pocketbook. My part-time job wasn't getting it and my stipend had been cut off. I called a job placement agency and secured a Human Resources position. This time I was moving up from an assistant to a specialist. How about them apples!! So this is why God sent me back to school, to equip and prepare me with something bigger and better.

I was making significantly more money than I had on my previous job, but I still wasn't fully content. I have to admit, my first day on the job went very well. As months went by, I developed friendships and really found myself excited about going to work. I was commuting between Winston Salem and Salisbury like I had done after having my daughter. Keeping it real, the money I poured into my gas guzzler was stretching my pockets.

There was one person in particular that God connected me to. He spoke to me that there would be a time I would need to minister to her. I thought, "ministering, who's going to do that?" Not me, I'm certainly not in a place where God could use me like that. I was all jacked up. I would come to learn that regardless of my status, God could use Even Me!

As time went by, I noticed that this young lady's mannerisms were very similar to mine. She was around the same age as my sister and would always ask a lot of questions about me. I began to talk to Christan more and more. We had so much in common that it was unreal. Her life stories were analogous to my life stories.

After a year, I thought of her as a little sister to me. We talked on our way to work and we would talk even more once we got there. Knowing we had plenty of work to do, our conversations would go on and on.

One day our supervisor decided to make some organizational changes. He paired employees throughout the office and Christan and I were assigned the same office space for a short time. Needless to say, we didn't get much work done. We spent our time talking and laughing. Our new roles began impacting the entire office. The morale was low and it was so quiet across the office that you could probably hear a pin drop on the carpet.

Around October, I started dreading the idea of going to work. My job was still pretty laid back. I'd moved back to my own office and there were still some co-workers who made coming to work worthwhile. I'd arranged a flexible work schedule that would soon come to an end.

I found myself sitting at my desk wishing that I could find a good enough reason to leave. I typed my resignation letter more than once but erased it and ripped up the hardcopy.

Around the holidays, my pastor preached on sermon topics like "Don't' Quit", and "Stay Where You Are" and things of that sort. Here I was trying to leave my job and that's what I had to hear on Sunday's.

Week after week I'd drag myself in the office, with the same feelings. Where was my bigger and better job?

By this time, Christan was expecting her first child and I was able to encourage her about life, the baby and what it is like being a single parent. Her consulting me and me encouraging her made the bond between us even tighter.

Life Interruption Four: Becoming Unemployed

"I had prayed and asked to be removed but when it was time for God to do it, I became frightened. "

I usually wake up to Good Morning America to see what is going on in the world. As usual, more layoffs, more houses in foreclosure and more banks in trouble. On one particular day, my mood was off; not something that I could describe. I was prepared for work, eager to see certain co-workers, even though going to work was something I really didn't want to do. When I arrived, the atmosphere was very dry. It felt like someone had opened their mouth and sucked all of the air out of the building.

It took me a while to get into my normal routine of checking emails, voicemail messages, and filing, etc. I received an instant message from my boss, "Alisha, can I talk to you for a minute?" What now? I thought. As I sat in his office, he began to fill me in on future cutbacks that were going to take place and my Human Resource position was on the list. He gave me three options to consider over the weekend: take a pay cut, assume another position in the office or go on a "supposedly" temporary layoff. I had a Master's in Business Administration wasn't making exactly what I thought I was worth and already dreaded going to work. It wasn't hard to select the layoff.

Let me fill you in, prior to receiving the instant message; I had been praying for a way out of that company. So, that sayin, "be careful what you ask for, you might just get it" was so on point. I had prayed and asked to be removed but when it was time for God to do it, I was frightened.

I had checked into what my unemployment benefits would consist of and had established a budget, for once, so that I could pay my bills accordingly. Wait a minute, now I have to cut back on shopping trips to Marshalls, Ross, Roses and the Goodwill? I have to go home and tell my daughter that I have been laid off? Knowing how much we enjoy going for pedicures and eating out. I had no clue about what I was going to do, or how I'm going to keep it together. A single parent with one income was now laid-off with very little income. What kept me calm was the fact that I wasn't the only one impacted by the layoff. So was my co-worker, the person who God had sent me to minister to, only she was pregnant.

My last day on that job was harder than I imagined. My co-workers took me out for lunch and it was rather bittersweet.

However; bondage had been broken but bonds had been made in this place. I had come in contact with some people who I really hope will remain in my life. After loading my belongings in the car, I sat there for a few minutes and I even shed a few tears because I knew this was the end and that God was not bringing me back to this place even if I was leaving for a "temporary "layoff.

As the days, weeks and months went by; I became a pro at filing my unemployment claim. There were only five questions the Employment Security Commission asked and each week my answers were: no, no, no, no, and yes. Where else can you go and give people answers like that without them coming back, wanting you to elaborate? For a minute I became spoiled with my little employment break. It was just what I needed though. Looking for a job was the last thing on my mind. I can sleep in, not punch a clock and get paid for doing absolutely nothing. I would get my daughter off to school, get back in the bed and chat with Christan for hours.

High Hopes

"Why can't we take what we have been exposed to, mix it with the knowledge that we have acquired and make it our own?"

One day Christan and I had a very unusual conversation about life. It wasn't until then that we recognized that we both had Bachelor's and Master's degrees. We were two highly intelligent women who knew we could do anything we put our minds to but we were sitting on the phone complaining about not having a job. There were plenty of area companies where we could put our degrees to use. We complained long and hard about our situation, but failed to put together a plan to change.

Later that afternoon, I went to a local dollar store and ran into a minister from my church, she joked with me about having the time to shop during the day. All of a sudden, her tone changed and she said, "Lish, you will not work for anyone else." I heard her words loud and clear. But what is it that I would find myself doing? I enjoy event planning and decorating. I like working with the at-risk youth, not to mention my previous Human Resources exposure. I still didn't know what the future held for me career wise. Particularly, I was destined to be self-employed, but, what am I going to do now? When I returned home I called Christan and shared with her what I thought we could possibly do. We were both good at our jobs. We knew what the client/ staff ratio looked like and how to secure resources and many of the other pertinent details. Maybe we could take what we'd been exposed to, mix it with the knowledge that we acquired in other roles and make it our own. Christan responded, "Yeah, yeah Lisha we can do that." Then she added that we could also do this and this and this. She suggested and I added to it. We had things mapped out to the "t"; but still hadn't consulted God about anything. We decided to go on a fast and meditate on Proverbs 3. Sad to say, but able to admit, He agreed with some of it; but not all if it.

Somewhere between getting frustrated, being unemployed, and the birth of a new baby, our motivation slowed down. We knew what we wanted to do but the pieces to the puzzle were not fitting together. We would write down ideas and toss them to the side. However, we had a plan, but had no money. Christan said, what business do you know of that runs off air?" We laughed like that was the funniest question she'd ever asked. But true indeed, she had a point. At the moment, paying bills became harder than normal and God knew that between the both of us, we didn't have any extra.

Dreams

"When the page came up, I saw these women from Chicago, IL with the same vision that God had given us except for they were walking in theirs."

I was running late for a meeting at the church where an impromptu video was going to be made when Christan called. All I heard was "you are not going to believe this" being said over and over again. Here I am thinking that something was wrong with the baby or she had just heard some bad news. "Go to the computer and type in Elect Lady", she shouted. Not knowing what to expect, but based upon the sound of her voice I was nervous and anxious at the same time. When the page came up, I saw these women from Chicago, IL with the same vision that God had given us except they were walking in theirs.

At that moment, I thought that God had turned his back on me once again. All I could think was, "God you gave this to us, so why are you altering the plan." Here is another one of those life interruptions that Bishop Eddie Long had preached about. As bad as I didn't want to question him, this time I demanded an explanation. Here I am ready to get endorsed, ready to file my Articles of Incorporation and now this. The feeling went right back to emptiness. I was already dealing with stress and depression and this go round one more blow probably would take me out. I called my best friend Teauana with the horrific news as well as some other friends who were aware of the idea that we had, complaining and crying at the same time. Teauana seemed to have been the calmest between the three of us. By the way, she's a nurse. So being calm is her specialty. She began to look at the website and all she could say was "Lish, WOW." She then later stressed that there were some extra components that we had that was missing from what the website showed. We can still make this work she added. My thoughts by this time were "yeah, I hear ya." Even though I received encouragement, I didn't want to hear what they were saying, they hadn't walked in my shoes and this pair didn't have any extra room in them.

Have you ever been so afraid to ask the Lord what next but you do anyway? Hoping and praying that He will hear you, but not answer, because you are afraid of what He will say. I tried with all I had in me to keep Christan encouraged because of where her hopes had reached. The ideas and visions that she had were just as grand as mine and Teauana's. I was so disappointed and angry with God because He allowed us to see and believe in visions that belonged to someone else. I asked God, "why would you reveal to me what your plan was for our life and then you take it back?"

Before going to bed that night I had to repent for being angry, then I had to get in a place where I could hear from God and no one else. Time went on and on still nothing. My thoughts by now were, "where in the world are You?" "Why are You leaving me hanging like this?" Did You forget that I just got delivered from some serious stuff, so that I could receive all that you have for me? "What more do You want me to do?" Still no answer. Life went on. No signs, no small still voice.

A few months later I woke up with a migraine; which was the worst kind to encounter. Here I am late for choir practice and then this lady called about a car that I had inquired about earlier. It was cold and raining outside. I wasn't sure about what to do at first; but I ended up skipping choir practice, called a friend to accompany me to Charlotte to look at a Cadillac Escalade. Bad choice! Knowing that I was already seeking God for answers and then what did I do? Put worshipping Him in spite of my migraine on the back burner.

When I arrived at the dealership, I saw the Cadillac Escalade that I was all hyped about, but it was all wrong, from the color to the size. When I got inside to go for a test drive, "Your Will" by Darius Brooks was playing. How many times have you been to a car dealership, get in a vehicle to go for a test drive and gospel is playing? Slim to none. While listening to the words, "I wish I could tell You just what I want" which is the Escalade "and You'll give it to me just like"; which I knew probably wasn't going to happen because God still hadn't answered the other questions. How ironic. The song goes on to say that "the truth of the matter what I want just might hurt me and You won't let me go out like that" I knew that if I traded the car that I had for the Escalade my car payment would increase, on top of that I am still unemployed; but I wanted an Escalade. Still listening to the song, the verse comes up, "So I'll cry till You tell me, let it go let it be, oh Lord Your will is what's best for me." So you know, by this time, I was crying inside because this car in particular was not part of the plan.

I didn't need any additional distractions to keep me from hearing from Him. Needless to say, I did not get the car instead I ended up having a migraine that lasted for four days straight. All I could do was sit and pray for relief. The meds that I had were either expired or just not working at all.

The following Sunday I filed my unemployment claim and received a message indicating that I had two weeks of benefits left. "What in the world?" I thought I was covered until February 2010. I called Christan and shared the news with her. What for? She just made matters worse with her whining and complaining; which caused me to whine and become upset.

I had to find a job. I applied for a couple of jobs but kept my mind on what had been prophesied to me. I really loved the idea of not working for anyone else. My thinking was interrupted by a call from Christan. Did you hear the news?

Obama is giving us another extension! "Thank you Lord" was all that I could say. When we hung up, I got in my receptive mode and started releasing the questions that I had for Him that day. Lord, what is up with this unemployment thing? Before I knew it, I had written down what I made when I was working and what I had received in unemployment. I added the two of them together and came up with the calculation of my worth; what I should have been making on the job that I was laid off from.

The knowledge that I had gained from working in Human Resources had equipped me enough to know what my worth was and where the ball had been dropped by my employer. There were too many times when I went to my boss inquiring about a raise and he shot it down. I settled for that because it was a job and I enjoyed the people that I worked with.

God revealed to me that He was already giving me what I was worth and that I didn't have to work for it. All I had to do was sit at home, answer a few questions and hit submit. That's what I call unmerited favor. I have heard about other people being blessed with things and having stuff to go their way. Not realizing that God will actually give you what you need and sometimes don't deserve, without even having to work for it. So you know I had to ask, Lord can that happen to Even Me? Yes, even you.

I started to feel better about the extended unemployment benefits. Then from nowhere God came with another school idea. I've had family members approach me and ask "What degree is this? How many do you have now? What are you doing with the one's you got? Words can cut you so deep that they penetrate and open up old wounds leaving you aching for life. Those wounds that Neosporin and a band-aids still can't heal. And God, You think that I want to go back to school and invest my time and emotions in another degree?

I had to get myself in a place to hear what He was instructing me to do. I had a dual Bachelors degree, a Masters degree and there was nothing left to pursue but my Doctorate. I am right back at square one. This was the original educational plan for my life, but God You sent me through all of this to bring me back to it?

While googling DBA and PhD programs, Walden University caught my attention. I ended up looking into a Doctor of Business Administration program. I called an enrollment specialist who was super nice to me. It seemed as if I was sitting in her office instead of talking to her on the phone. She informed me that the program consisted of 60 semester credit hours. I responded "Nah, that's ok. I don't have time to do all that." She then asked about my Masters degree. To my surprise, since I had a Master of Business Administration, I only had to complete 27 hours instead of 60, which was 9 classes and two residencies instead of a dissertation.

I thought, I might be able to handle that. I got all set up and prepared myself for Walden University. "Dr. Byrd sounds pretty good to me," I thought. I can work with it; but what is God going to do with it? Here is another degree and I am still unemployed.

Not long after I registered for my first residency I started dealing with stress and depression again. The stress was so bad that I went from 147 lbs. to 124 lbs in a matter of 4 months. I would wake up hungry, fix a rather large breakfast and get full off half of a boiled egg.

Finding clothes to wear became the most painful task because everything that I had in my closet was too big. I had to recreate clothes just to make a descent outfit. I had a closet full of size 8 & 10 clothes; but needed a size 2.

There were times, more than few when seeing the outside was something that I wasn't excited about. I would rather stay at home and sleep than to go out and be questioned by friends and family about my weight loss, because according to me I was "just fine." It's funny how when I was 147 lbs., they picked at the weight that I gained. Some even thought that I was pregnant.

The entire time I was in denial about what I was dealing with. I finally made a doctor's appointment because my weight loss was really starting to get the best of me. I knew that I had to get some help and let the things that were stressing me out, go.

While dealing with depression, it was time to start my second set of classes. At this point, my motivation level was slim to none. I ended up dropping one of my classes, not knowing that it was going to affect my student loan. I needed that money to pay for my residency and other expenses for that week. However, I still needed help. I started looking into flights since my residency was being held in Atlanta. I was able to find a few that were at a descent price range.

A dear friend of mine knew that this was a trip that I needed to go on, just to get away and knew that I really didn't have the money to pay for my flight. To my surprise, he put just enough money under my doormat to cover some of my expenses. Yes, I thought, I can still get away for a few days. Needless to say, one day later the prices and the times of the flights had changed. I was discouraged, frustrated, and angry all at once. Yes I was! I was all of those things because I needed to get away to clear my head. Not just for the residency, but for my sanity. A week later while in the shower, I started praying about my residency. I could hear God telling me "YOU CAN'T GO." Can't go? Lord, I really need to get away from here to clear my mind. And he said it again, "YOU CAN'T GO." By this time I was more upset than ever.

Life Interruption Five
The death of Monica

"Before we got off the phone, the last words that Monica always spoke to me were; "I Love You Byrd" and I responded with "I Love You More."

Right when I am trying to trust the Lord with all my heart, He takes a love one out of my life again. My mom called me the day after I was scheduled to attend my residency with some news that literally knocked me off my feet. Her words were "Lish, did you hear about Monica?" One my close girlfriends who had been sick had just died. Losing Monica was like losing a sister. We had been very close friends for eighteen years. I was the first friend that she made when she moved to Salisbury and we established a bond that was unbreakable.

Two weeks before she died we conversed for an hour about

life, our children and her illness. This conversation was a bit different from the ones that we had in the past. Usually, someone was always at her house or our conversation would be cut short. We would talk for a few minutes here and there but this time we talked for an hour. The laughter that came through the phone was laughter that I hadn't heard since high school. I was amazed at how much strength she had gained since the last time we spoke to each other. I was so happy for her, and her family, and even happier to hear where God had brought her from.

Even though Monica and I lived in different cities we kept each other updated on the things that were going on around us. Halfway through the conversation, we talked about our fifteenth year high school class reunion scheduled that year. We looked forward to seeing everyone. Monica told me that if she had to come with her oxygen mask she would be there.

After giggling like school girls, there was a sudden shift in the conversation. It was then that we began talking about her illness. This was a subject that we avoided most of the time so that we could have a normal conversation. I tried to always remain unmovable about her condition, even though I was sadden by what she was going through. Monica shared with me the "big news"; she had been placed on the lung transplant list and awaiting a call from Duke Hospital with the go ahead to receive a new lung. Everything was finally working out in her favor. Her long battle with Sarcoidosis was about to be over. In addition, the prayers that had been prayed by many as well as her own were finally being answered. Monica had accepted what she was going through and she had accepted Christ which made her trails and tribulations easier to bear.

"Enough about me Byrd, what's going on with you?" she asked. I mentioned to her that I had been dealing with stress and depression. I started complaining about this and that, in a matter of minutes she stopped me and told me that I need to let it go. "Stress was one of the things that caused my sickness; little do you know, I would love to walk in your shoes right now" she stated. "Byrd, let it go, stress and worrying over things that you have little or no control over is not worth it, give it to God and let Him work it out." Hearing those words were piercing because I was complaining to a woman whose condition was not only worse than mine, but she was fighting for her life. Those words, at that moment and especially after her death, changed my life. So many times we are quick to complain that we never take time during our complaining to consider that somebody, somewhere is dealing with situations and circumstances that are far worse than our own. Before we got off the phone, the last words that Monica always spoke to me were "I Love You Byrd" and I responded with "I Love You More". Those are 4 words that I will forever cherish and words that I don't take lightly when sincerely spoken to me.

As the days went by, and as the time was approaching for Monica's funeral, my body was still somewhat numb and I was still in shock from the fact that she was really gone. I had to find extra activities to keep my mind occupied. My closest girlfriends and I prepared ourselves for Monica's funeral. I am aware of the fact that I saw her lying there but I was still trying to comprehend how losing Monica happened in a matter of two weeks. At the end of the service, the Funeral Director informed us that Monica came to him three years prior and made all of her funeral arrangements.

I remember questioning God about why her, especially when she was so close to her healing. After hearing about how she took care of her earthly business before she died brought about an inner peace within myself that I know she had within hers. Monica had allowed herself to have a relationship with God that granted her peace that surpassed all understanding. At that moment and at that time was when I thanked God for her struggle being over and for a life well lived. Remembering the good times will always penetrate my mind and reside in my heart.

I said all of that to say this, God knew that He was going to take Monica home during the time that I was supposed to be away. He knew that after receiving the news about her death that I would not have been able to concentrate on completing my residency. Now I understand why he said "You can't go". My daily prayer has been "God grant me the Serenity to Accept the things I cannot Change, Courage to Change the things I can and the Wisdom to know the difference". In the midst of life's interruptions, I needed all of those things: serenity, acceptance, change, courage and wisdom.

Throughout the years, I have been wearing a mask that hid the emptiness from being a fatherless child, becoming a single parent, losing Uncle John, being laid-off from my job, and losing a close friend; but God would not allow me to give up on the vision that he had given me. Of course I had to ask, God with all of this going on, you still want to use EVEN ME? Yes, even you!

Part Two

*Once Broken:
A Mended Heart*

Minister Tina, my pastor's wife introduced the ladies in our church to a book by Paula White entitled *"Deal With It: You Cannot Conquer What You Will Not Confront"*. Minister Tina called me one night and asked me to be a leader for a group. Me? I asked. At first I was hesitant, but eventually said yes. Minister Tina mentioned that five ladies were in our group and we were to read, study and discuss the Leah Chapter. Not knowing who Leah was in the bible or what her story was about, I skipped over Ruth which was the first chapter and went straight to Leah.

The subheading was "If I could just find Prince Charming to love me...." "This is going to be rather interesting?" I thought. I've always found myself being in some of the most questionable, longest and weirdest relationships. According to me, they were just what I thought I needed. I received the attention and a little extra from these "so called" relationships which caused me look for love in all the wrong places, and allowed me to cover up my "emptiness". It didn't dawn on me till my early thirties that I had settled so much when it came to men. Talking about worth and self esteem gone out the door! Not knowing that there was a need to be something more than just a reflection of a man.

I had so much in common with Leah that it was unreal. I thought that I needed a man to notice me, take heed to what I was saying and become acquainted with me. Completely clueless to the fact that the only man I needed to do those things was God.

I wanted a man to notice the inner beauty that was hidden beneath the scars and the brokenness. I wanted them to see beyond my light skin tone. I wanted them to pick up on the hurt in my eyes without me saying a word. I wanted them to see beyond the car that I drove and the designer this and that, that I wore. In reality that was a task that was hard to accomplish. Undoubtedly, all they wanted to see was what was beneath the skinny jeans and Victoria Secret garments that I wore and the heart that I unselfishly gave. I craved their attention and yes of course, they desired mine.

Church Hurt

I got wrapped up in one friendship that I thought could potentially have been headed toward a relationship. I met this man in particular when I was still wrapped up in another man. This man wanted me to see him, hear him, and know him. When I didn't even see, hear, or know myself.

We spent countless hours on the phone for days which turned into weeks and months. He informed me that he didn't like getting involved with women in the church who had children because they would often time try to push their kids off on him. After getting to know me a little better and after seeing that I was different from that category of women, he became interested in knowing my likes and dislikes, as well as my dreams. We chatted more and more frequently, by then my thoughts were, Where in the world was God hiding him? This man was willing to do things that I have always wanted to do and everything in between. He knew how to use the correct jargon that was spoken at the right time and knew how to throw in Godly principles to keep my attention. We went out on a couple of dates, and found ourselves getting closer, then one day he admitted that there was another woman that he was also attracted to. "This was a joke," I thought. I have been dating a man who was dipped in gold and trimmed in silver. I had been so wrapped up his camouflage that I became a chameleon feeling like I really mattered. You mean to tell me that I wasn't the only woman that he wanted to feel this way? Still unaware of the magnitude of the situation, I welcomed the opportunity to find out who the other woman was.

To my surprise the very woman who prophesied to me about never working again was the same woman who served as his little "secret". I was hurt by his actions but I was deeply scarred because that woman, a minister at that who witnessed my deliverance, ministered to me and prayed over me was his secret. I found myself questioning the motives of a minister. Had this minister used her gifting of ministry as a strength towards his weakness? From my understanding this secret had been going on all along. The whole time I had been thinking that it was all about me. According to him, this minster was reaching places and pouring into him spiritually where I hadn't. This so called pouring felt good to his flesh and made him want more of it which caused an attraction between the two of them.

Even though I knew what had transpired, he apologized and said he still wanted to be with me. I was desperate for companionship and allowed him to come back. We went on as if nothing had happened until another confession surfaced.

While I thought they were over; they were still seeing each other and the supposedly attraction was still there.

I cried so much at night that I felt like I could've drank my tears for water so that I could stay hydrated. I told myself that I was not going back to the church that I had been in for 20 years because I was not strong enough to sit in the same church with them. I was determined not to go back there simply because of church hurt. Merely because I thought that I would not be able to hear her pray or preach a sermon and be receptive to it being from God and not woman.

I was ready to run forgetting that I was there first. I could not allow two new members who have hurt my feelings, run me out of a church that I had grown up in and received so much spiritual food from. I prayed and prayed to God about what I needed to do and how I had to conduct myself. His words for me were "Let it Go". Letting it go was a hard pill to swallow because I had become comfortable with experiencing newness. I had become open, to feeling wanted once again. I had become seen, heard and known all over again and it felt good. But the truth of the matter is that right then that was not part of God's will for me.

While allowing God to prepare me to let go and leave this dark path is when I learned that my destiny is etched in my trail of tears and that the soon to be dry tear stains will eventually symbolize the path where the smiles of my healing are formed.

I will admit that I was extremely hurt by the mess that God had exposed me to but I was grateful of the fact that beyond needing to be seen, heard, and known, that I was able to praise God for bringing me out of the lies, the deception, the filth, and the blind spots.

God allowed me to go through this temporary hurt and pain so that I could notice Him, take heed to what He was saying, and become reacquainted with Him and Him only. God allowed me to come out of this situation as better woman than when I went in. God allowed me to walk through the fire without being consumed. I learned to hold my head up in the midst of hurt and pain and to remain focused on His grace, mercy and peace while I sat in church, under the same roof as them. God allowed me to smile during the times when I wanted to cry. God allowed me to realize that no weapon formed against me shall prosper. God prepared me to reap the benefits from acknowledging Him. I was able to release the past and stand firm on His promises and purpose for my future. This was not my first time overcoming opposition and adversity. I made a promise that I would start living my life like its golden. I had to stop settling for the silver and bronze and wait for the real gold that God has for me. I declared that I am a virtuous woman who knows how to praise God in spite of what I go through; knowing that He still wants to use EVEN ME.

Being a daddy's girl was what I always wanted to be. I wanted to have a dad who would give me everything that I asked for. I wanted to be kissed on the forehead after falling off my bike. I even wanted him to scare off the boy who picked me up for the prom. I wanted him to buy me a lavish car when I turned sixteen. You see, I said I wanted and not I needed. What I really wanted and needed was far beyond the materialistic things that money could easily buy. In actuality, all I really needed was for him to love me unconditionally, which would have eliminated the love that I desperately searched for in other places. These were the desires that I had but were far beyond my reach because my daddy wasn't there; but other men were. My mother's husband, who is now deceased, tried his hardest to give and do those things for me. He tried to fill in the blanks to make me happy and I am forever grateful for that. Once he died, clinging on to men who continued to do those things became a stronghold.

When I think about being broken, I am suddenly reminded

about Humpty Dumpty who had a great fall and wasn't able to be put together again. Then I think about my life and how broken I had been for years, the good thing about the brokenness that I experienced was that God was willing and able to mend every broken piece in spite of the sins that I openly committed.

Grace

And forgive your people, who have sinned against you; forgive all the offenses they have committed against you, and cause their conquerors to show them mercy.
1 King 8:50

"I never told my dad that I forgave him for not being there; but I have told God and have left it in His hands. I hope and pray that wherever he is that he knows that. "

Forgiveness

Part I

I received a phone call from my dad seven years ago, on Father's Day to be exact. He informed me that he had died and some friends rushed him to the hospital allowing enough time to be necessitated. He has a pace maker and has been dealing with a bad heart for years.

I was moved by the fact that he was still dealing with heart issues. I was also moved by the fact that he felt that I was worthy enough to know about the situation. After we hung up, I had to ask God to forgive me for carrying animosity around in my heart for all these years. I never told my dad that I forgave him for not being there; but I have told God and have left it in his hands. I hope and pray that wherever he is that he knows that.

Even though I wanted him in my life, I was still angry with the fact that he chose not to be. Being able to forgive someone who has never had the decency to say "I'm sorry" is a serious thing. I am determined to never let a person regardless of who they are, rob me of my peace nor keep me from prospering. I want all that God has for me and in order to receive it, I have to forgive those who have abused, misused and wronged me.

"For years, I carried so much animosity in my heart towards a man who actually wanted to do right by his child."

Part II

During my senior year in high school I met a guy while working at my part-time job. I thought he was cute, among other things. We hit it off and started dating. He took me to my senior prom and we remained a couple after high school. We both went off to college and I found myself being at his school more than my own. Our relationship at the time appeared to be going somewhere. He showed me the attention that I craved and I gave him the same in return.

During my junior year of college, I got pregnant and our lives changed instantly. We became parents at the age of 20 and 21. Although we had no clear direction for life, but it was what it was. Our relationship went down hill from there and I was at home raising our child and back to feeling empty. Empty because I thought that having a baby was going to keep him around not push him away. I gave this man a child but wanting me was no longer in his plans. I was convinced that we were going to get married after college and raise our daughter together in the same home. I was certain that what I had experienced with my dad was not going to happen to my daughter. We were able to make the proper decisions for our daughter but I was hurt because I did not want to be a single parent. I didn't want to be unattractive to men because I had a child. And I most definitely did not want to be looked down upon by church folk. This hurt made me angry and bitter. It made me act unlady like at times and it turned me into a woman that I didn't recognize. For years, I carried so much animosity in my heart towards a man who actually wanted to do right by his child. It wasn't until we both established a better relationship with God that he was able to apologize for the hurt that had been caused and I was able to accept it and forgive him and myself.

"I stayed on my knees constantly praying for those individuals as much as I did for myself."

Part III

The man and woman who were previously discussed in *church hurt* really caused me to be a better person. For days, weeks and months I didn't have the strength to hold my head up due to the hurt that I had experienced. I had to come to the realization that if God can bring me to it, He can bring me through it.

I stayed on my knees constantly praying for those individuals as much as I did for myself. I had to keep reminding myself that yes, she ministered, prophesied and witnessed my deliverance; but my deliverance did not come from her, it came from God.

I have forgiven both of them just like God has forgiven me for the many sins that I have committed. Releasing them has broken bondage and dried every tear from my eyes.

Mercy

Yet give attention to your servant's prayer and his plea for mercy, O LORD my God. Hear the cry and the prayer that your servant is praying in your presence this day.
 1 Kings 8:28 (NIV)

"That day I asked them to pray for me and I begged God to deliver me from what was not of Him because I was tired of the woman I had become by settling for less than what was meant for me."

Deliverance

I met a man about ten years ago who was attractive, charming, carried himself well and married. We became friends and friends turned into a relationship, a breakup and heartache. He eventually became separated and later divorced, by this time we were on a more serious level, well at least that's what I thought. I was so wrapped up in how he made me feel that I could care less about his ex-wife and children who were getting hurt in the process. When I say his actions and ways took me there, they sure did. They took me to exotic trips to Cancun and Jamaica and right back to that feeling called emptiness at times. Never realizing that the desire of a man that I was craving, was what I was longing to have from my dad: feeling loved, cherished and wanted.

This entanglement lasted for ten whole years. Even after the restoration, I went back to settling, lost my dignity and portions of myself worth because after the breakups and heartaches, he still made me feel like I wanted to feel. He continued to fill that empty place in my life where my father didn't dwell. Throughout the years, we established a bond that was so tight that no matter what you used you couldn't untie it. We eventually went our separate ways, but the friendship was still unbreakable.

It wasn't until I was invited to a retreat hosted by some women from my church that I realized that I was ready for change. We had devotion, ate lunch, and then got on the subject of *Soul Ties*. I had heard about the book but never read it. They broke the book down so well to where I knew I didn't have to buy it. I came to the realization that I had been caught up in some serious things. That day I asked them to pray for me and I begged God to deliver me from what was not of Him because I was tired of the woman I had become by settling for less than what was meant for me.

I was tired of being distracted and not being able to hear His actual plan for my life. I wanted to be delivered from the unclean ways and thoughts that were keeping me from having that real relationship with Him. It was that day that I turned it over to Him and got delivered from the bondage that was robbing me of my joy and peace. It was that day that I had my first real personal encounter with God. The feeling that I felt was so indescribable. When I got off the floor I felt as if I had been emptied out. My eyes were so sore from crying that a nap was the next best thing for me. That very real, personal encounter with God was so amazing and so powerful. It was that day when I was able to say that I had been delivered and

I was ready and I mean ready to be used by God. When I was out there in the world I didn't think that God could empty out and pour back into, disinfect, purify and use ME!

Peace

Don't worry about anything; instead, pray about everything. Tell God what you need, and thank Him for all He has done. Then you will experience God's peace, which exceeds anything we can understand. His peace will guard your hearts and minds as you live in Christ Jesus.
Phillipians 4:6-7 (NLV)

"He allowed God to lead him to touch some places in my heart and life that only God will be able to reward him for."

Restoration

I have been in so many relationships that God said "leave alone" or just plain "no" to. But you know how we get sometimes, we want to test the waters anyway. As I sit back and think about the mess that I got caught up in, I thank God for sending a man my way who restored me in ways he couldn't have planned for.

I had been down in the dumps for months over a relationship that had gone bad. One Thanksgiving Eve, I was on the phone talking to my best friend Teauana while shopping at Wal-Mart. Out of the blue, this handsome man that I had never seen before not only caught my eye, but ended up on most of the same isles I was on. We spoke and kept it moving. It seemed as if he was following me. Teauana and I continued our conversation as I described to her how he looked and how nice the sports jersey was that he wore.

After I left, he asked one of the cashiers who I was. She didn't know my name but she knew what church I belonged to. Two weeks later, he showed up at my church. We made eye contact but didn't speak. We didn't officially meet until two weeks later. He was very easy on the eye and had a smile to die for. We exchanged numbers and later spoke about life, careers, and our families. He had been in Salisbury for three years, living five miles away from me and our paths never crossed. The way that he traveled to his house was similar to the way that I went home. There were all types of connections that could have brought us together, and unknowingly, we knew many of the same people. His son was enrolled at the same school that my cousin worked at. I mentioned to her that I had met him and she told me that he was a very nice man and an involved parent.

Our paths never crossing before then remind me of Ecclesiastes 3. "A Time for Everything." I have been persuaded that to everything there is a season. There are times when Gods seasons for us are opposite than the regular winter, spring, summer and fall seasons that we are accustomed to. I would not have ever thought that after a dry summer that joy would have had enough room to get through.

While getting to know each other, he introduced me to *Covergirls* written by TD Jakes. This book was a page turner and became hard for me to put down. Unknowingly to him, it was what I needed during the time. We continued to have conversations and opened up about what had gone on in our past. There were times when I felt like he could see straight through me because he knew where to take the conversation, penetrate the hurt, and then speak words of encouragement to heal it. He allowed God to lead him to touch some places in my heart and life that only God will be able to reward him for. God sent me a Boaz minded man that looked beyond my scars, mended the brokenness, noticed my heart, and valued my worth. After getting to know him a little better, he informed me that he was going to be stationed overseas for four years. On the eve of his departure I asked him if I could have the sports jersey that I saw him in the very first time. To my surprise, he gave it to me and I still have it in my closet to this day.

Before he left he asked "Once I get settled, if I send for you will you come?" Yeah right I thought. He will get there and forget all about me. One month after he left, on Mother's Day morning to be exact, he called to let me know that he had made it safely and to wish me a Happy Mother's Day. Before getting off the phone he asked "When can you come and how long can you stay"? I almost hit the floor. This man was actually sincere about me visiting him. I looked at my calendar made the necessary arrangements for my daughter and took a two week vacation in Europe. Once I got there and got settled in, this Boaz minded man treated me with the utmost respect. I felt like the real Cinderella. He respected the woman that he met in the states as well as the woman who had traveled over 6,000 miles alone. I always told myself that I was going to write a book titled *The Joy That Winter Brings*. Not knowing that I would be able to write about it in *Even Me*. Moreover, whenever I find myself in tough situations, I can always talk to the Boaz minded man that God sent to water and nurture those dead and dry areas in my life. I am at a place of peace and I am so grateful that God could use a man besides himself to continuously restore EVEN ME!

Favor

My Aunt Chris gave me a card when I received my Master's Degree about starting off with baby steps, becoming a little girl and then transitioning into a young woman. Even as a baby, a little girl and as a young woman, God's favor was upon me all along. At the end she wrote, we are blessed because you are blessed.

I am blessed not because of who I am; but because of whose I am. Just because of the blessings that are upon me; my people will be blessed as well.

"He spoke to me so loud and plain that a deaf man would have been able to hear."

God's Master Plan

I was listening to "Your Will" by Darius Brooks this time, I was focusing on "I will cry till you tell me let it go let it be" I heard those words from God before, remember the Escalade that I wanted? While listening to the song I started looking for a song that I heard on BET's Sunday's Best but I didn't know the name. I clicked on the first song that came up. The songstress ministered "Even Me". I put that song on repeat because it sounded so good.

I was on Day 30 of *30 Thoughts for Victorious Living* by Joel Osteen, a book that someone had shared with me and the thought for the day was "Praise Him for the Victory". Earlier that morning I did just that, thanked Him for victory. Even though I didn't have my Escalade, even though I was unemployed, even tough I still hadn't heard back from Him about my vision; I praised him anyway. There was one line in the book that caught my attention, "Quit worrying and start worshiping! Start praising and thanking God, and expect things to change in your favor".

I went in my home office and started making copies of certain pages of the book so that I could return it back to the person who loaned it. While listening to the song, I asked God once again about Elect Ladies. He directed me to a picture that my mom and sister gave me called "Crowns of Glory". There are three women in this picture; one of grace, one of mercy and one of peace (that Bishop Eddie Long preached about in a sermon).

His words to me were "who are you and who are they?" God pointed out that this is Teauana, Christan and me. Based upon the year that I have been having, I knew that peace had to be mine. Then I started dwelling on the colors. I found out what red, gold, and green meant from a worldly and biblical standpoint. Once I put one and two together I can tell which one is Teauana and Christan. "No you can't, only they can tell who they are", I had to tell myself. While concentrating on this project, God kept speaking about switching things around. This time he gave me specific instructions, not partial instructions. "Here we go again," I started thinking. What now?

In the meantime of Him not answering me back, I emailed Teauana and Christan what I had put together and told them to figure out which one they were. Christan bless her heart was torn between good 'ol grace and mercy and Teauana seemed to have been lost for words. As bad as I knew I needed all three, God knew that I needed peace more. While allowing them enough time to ponder upon where they were in life, I listened to more calming music and told God that I am all yours, talk to me and He did just that.

Lish, you have to let parts of Elect Ladies go so that I can do a greater work in you. You need to write a book. Just like chicken soup is good for the soul, so is laughter and that's just what I did. Laughed! Not long after that I allowed myself to get in a receptive mode so that I could hear what He was talking about. I put my headphones on, continued to listen to "Even Me" and cried like a baby.

Within minutes He spoke to me so loud and plain that a deaf man would have been able to hear. He pinpointed some things that occurred during prior weeks and explained how and why they happened. "Now you have the opportunity to get it right this time so do it. I am going to take you back to some places, so get ready and enjoy the ride". I grabbed my notebook and a pen and wrote the vision as He gave it to me. The rest of that night I was unable to sleep because of all the excitement from hearing what he was speaking to me. When I found a stopping point, I closed my eyes to get a wink of sleep and here he comes again. Add this, add that, and write this down. Before I knew it, it was four o'clock in the morning and I was still writing the vision as He was instructing me on how to make it plain.

By the time I closed my eyes, my alarm was going off for me to wake my daughter up. It's time for me to take my daughter to school and I have only had three hours of sleep.

I was still so excited about what had been given to me, that I went to the bathroom, saw my eyes were red and swollen from the lack of sleep and from crying from the encounter that I had with God that night. As I was looking at myself in the mirror, He spoke to me yet again, "this is just the beginning, and you will have many more nights like this". Encounters like this with You? I asked. EVEN ME? Yes, even you.

By this time I was thinking watch out Stella, Lish got her groove back!

An Answered Prayer

The night before the interview I called my Aunt Mae for some last minute support. Her words to me were "Thank God for your new job because it's yours."

Day after day I wake up praying that God would bless me with a job. Being unemployed had become rather old. Living off barely half of what I used to make was different. By no means am I complaining, I was ready for a change.

On one particular day, I woke up asking God to prepare me for the harvest that he had in store for me. I opened my bible and meditated on Psalms 55:22 and Galatians 6:9. After reading these scriptures I took a shower, still praying and believing that God would do exactly what I had just read. When I returned to my room a green light was flashing on my instant messenger. There was a message from a church member asking if I knew someone looking for a Human Resource Coordinator job. It seemed like a joke. I replied letting her know I was interested and had prior experience. I don't know who was most excited, her or me. I sent her my resume and was scheduled for an interview by the end of the day. Before the day was over, the devil attacked me so badly that I started to become discouraged and was ready to act in my flesh. Right when God is ready to bless me; the devil gets mad.

Two days before the interview I received a call saying that at first there were four applicants scheduled for interviews and now it was down to one, me! The night before the interview I called my Aunt Mae for some last minute support. Her words to me were "Thank God for your new job because it's yours." That alone was enough to go off on. Before going to bed I read Psalms 55:22 and Galatians 6:9 again.

By recasting my burdens on the Lord and refusing to give up, I'm reaping a harvest from an interview that I arrived for on Friday morning at 10:00 and left out of at 11:00. I was offered the job that I did not apply for at 12:45pm to start the following Monday at 8:15am.

I was so excited about the things that God had done that I had to share it with my family and church family. The following Sunday I gave the Offertory Appeal. The Offertory Appeal is when a person is asked to read a scripture and elaborate on it. I came prepared that morning, with everything typed up that I wanted the people to hear. While standing in the choir loft, I heard God telling me, "this is one time you have to be transparent." "Transparent about what I thought." The spirit was so high that morning. I was still trying to figure out what He was talking about. "Talk about the real condition, tell my people how you really feel". Here I am about to be in tears because I didn't want people in my business, especially church members. Some of my family members knew what I was going through, but the majority of the one's who belonged to my church, including my mother, didn't. When it came time for me to stand before the congregation, I reverted right back to the scriptures that I had been meditating on that week, Psalms 55 and Galatians 6:9. I began to tell the congregation how I thought that my burden was being unemployed, when in fact my burden was dealing with depression. I explained how the people in this very church had hurt my feelings by questioning me about the weight that I had lost. I also informed them that God moved my condition without moving me. I later told them about the job that God had blessed me with. When service was over, church members encouraged me and told me that they were moved by the struggles that I had dealt with; but they were more moved by the fact that I allowed God to use me in such a profound way.

That day was life changing because God took me to a place that I had never been before. He delivered me from some serious hurt and pain and my life is better for it.

When I arrived on my new job the atmosphere was different from the last job. It felt as if this was where I belonged. My boss was down to earth, laid back but, still professional. She had decorated the office with many of the sayings and words of encouragement that I like and have throughout my house. I am a big fan of the Live, Love, Laugh saying and so is she.

I sat at my desk, and I opened the top drawer to see what was inside. I ran across a few pens and note pads, the regular office stuff. In the very back of the drawer was a CD that was turned upside down. When I turned it over it said

"God's Elect Lady". I almost fell out my chair. I was in awe for a while. I started texting those who knew about the CD, the vision and the plan. I was trying my hardest not to start crying. When my boss came in I shared with her what I had found, the "Elect Lady" tag that I had on the front of my car and how it all pertained to me. All she could say was "you are here for a reason." As the day progressed, I put the CD in the computer to see if it was the same CD that I had at home, yes indeed, it was Bishop Eddie Long with the same message. "God what are you about to do in this place and what are you about to do in my life?" were the questions running through my mind.

As time progressed, my boss and I realized that we had much in common. To hear her constantly saying that I was sent there for a reason has made going to work rather easy. I wake up in the morning thanking God for sending me to a place where He dwells. For putting me in an atmosphere where I am comfortable. And He blessed me with a job that I hadn't applied for. Now that's FAVOR.

Two months after giving the offertory appeal, I went inside a gas station to pay for some gas. While standing at the coffee machine, this woman comes up to me and says, "I was at church the day you gave your testimony. I want you to know that your testimony has been my motivation." She started crying while telling me about being laid off for a year. "If God can bless you and others with a job like that, he can sure bless me." After agreeing with what she had just spoken, I told her that God is molding you and equipping you for something better; but you have to get yourself in a receptive mode so that you can hear him and allow him to do just that. The truth of the matter is as Christians, we never know who is watching us and actually listening. This woman remembered the exact words that I had spoken that day. I was so moved by the fact that my being obedient to become transparent, caused someone to become motivated and not give up. I continued going to work with a smile on my face and thanksgiving in my heart. The job that started off as a temporary later became permanent and I am still grateful for the things that He has done and will do.

Part Three

Now Worthy:
The Fruits Of The Spirit

"No rubies, and no diamonds, no silver or no pearls. There are some lessons that I had to learn that I would not trade in for this world. You told me that my trials only come to make me strong. And with this You promised, You promised never to leave me alone. Lord Your will is what's best for me". "Your Will" by Darius Brooks

Beneath the scars and brokenness, God allowed me to see not only the value but how worthy I really am. Not because I'm beautiful; not because I'm educated; not because of the materialistic things that I have. I'm worthy because a man by the name of God took the time to pour into, nurtured and flourished an unworthy vessel named Alisha. God used an imperfect person to pray me through and witness my deliverance so that he could perfect what was already living on the inside of me. God emptied me out, stripped me of all my impurities and filled me with the fruits of the spirit. The following fruits: love, joy, patience, kindness, goodness, faithfulness, gentleness and self-control are not cheap to buy, especially from the one who paid for them for us. We must not forget nor take for granted what cost Him so much.

Love

Charity suffereth long, and is kind; charity envieth not; charity vaunteth not itself, is not puffed up. Doth not behave itself unseemly, seeketh not her own, is not easily provoked, thinketh no evil. Rejoiceth not in iniquity, but rejoiceth in the truth. Beareth all things, believeth all things, hopeth all things, endureth all things.
1 Corinthians 13:4-7 (KJV)

Love to me is a tender word because it is something that I so desperately craved, gave, and abused. I was always eager to love others when I didn't take the time necessary to love myself. My makeup would be flawless; my hair was always in place, and I made it my business to match from head to toe. The outer appearance was all together but the inside was jacked up. If I was told how good I looked, how intelligent I was, and that I had my stuff together, I had a tendency to forget where those compliments could lead.

It wasn't until after I got freed from some sinful acts that I had indulged in and then delivered from the rest that I realized what agape love meant. Regardless of what has happened in your life, when you can extend charity to someone who has hurt you or wronged you, you're experiencing agape love.

Joy

Restore unto me the joy of thy salvation;
and uphold me with thy free spirit.
Psalms 51:12 (KJV)

"Though I may have walked in the shaking and trembling of the earthquake, I am still standing in the aftermath because I still have joy. " No one can say it better than Pastor Shirley Caesar. This joy that I have the world didn't give it to me and the world can't take it away. Having joy means that I can give God thanks in all situations, during the good and the bad.

Patience

And beside this, giving all diligence, add to your faith virtue; and to virtue knowledge; And to knowledge temperance; and to temperance patience; and to patience godliness; And to godliness brotherly kindness; and to brotherly kindness charity. For if these things be in you, and abound, they make you that ye shall neither be barren nor unfruitful in the knowledge of our Lord Jesus Christ.
2 Peter: 1-8

Career/Education

Out of all of the fruits of the spirit, patience has been the one that had a great impact on my life. It started when I graduated with my MBA. I really thought that with the credentials that I had, my salary was going to increase and all that good stuff. Once I got laid-off, I was under the assumption that I would be able to find a job right off the bat once again because of my credentials. There were times when I really wanted to rush things. At times I found myself trying to hurry what God had for me. I wanted it right then and there.

Companionship

I was impatient when it came to relationships. I saw how happy my friends and my sister were in their marriages and that caused me to want a man in my life so that I could get married. I was tired of being alone and wanted to experience the same thing. God had to pull the rug from under my feet in order to get my attention. First, God turned my supposedly six month temporary unemployment into nine months.

Secondly, God removed a man that I had become comfortable with so that He could prepare me for the harvest that was in store for me. I have become a "happily hidden" woman, meaning that I have stopped concentrating on looking for a man and have become so deeply hidden and protected by Christ.

When the one man that God has for me emerges, He will have to seek and go through Christ in order to find me. God is going to give me a man who will enhance me and not have to be enhanced. God is going to bless me with a mate who will be able to teach, not need to be taught, and God is going to bless me with a man who will thank God daily for keeping as worthy a woman as myself for a worthy man.

Kindness

*She openeth her mouth with wisdom; and
in her tongue is the law of kindness.
Psalms 31:26*

I have never considered myself as being an unkind person. When my family and friends call upon me for help, I have a hard time saying "no". I believe in helping people when I can. However, being too kind and always doing for people who have the same capabilities and resources as yourself can set you up to be a crutch. I remember being at church one Saturday for a "Deal With It" presentation. The group presenting was Dorcas which dealt with overload. Dorcas was one who found herself taking care of everyone besides herself. Her inability to say no caused her to die at an early age. Reesee, one of the presenters in the group explained how she related to Dorcas because she had always been the one in her family that everyone wanted a piece of. She stated,

"When you ask me to do something and I tell you no, don't take it to heart, just know that I am saying yes to myself." The statement that she made stuck with me for months, not only because it was the truth but because I saw myself in what had been spoken.

Not only, we as women, but we as a people take on too much all of the time. We have to allow ourselves to be taken care of instead of taking care of everybody and everything. I have come to the realization that I can be kind to people by leading them to the proper resources without doing the job for them. I can instruct someone on, not just how it works for me but how it can work for them if they are willing to put forth the effort to do the work. I pray that when I am approached by someone asking for my help for something that I know they can do themselves, not take it personal when I say "no." I have to acknowledge that I am saying "yes" to myself. I don't want to die at an early age because of overload.

Goodness

Surely goodness and mercy shall follow me all the days of my life: and I will dwell in the house of the LORD for ever.
Psalm 23:6 (KJV)

Goodness allows us to be loved, liked and enjoyed while reciprocating those exact things to others even if the devil almighty comes against us. Goodness allows us to be good to people who use and abuse us. When people wrong you or hurt you, continue to be good to them so that God' s goodness and mercy can follow you everywhere you go.

Faithfulness
A Living Sacrifice to God

And so, dear brothers and sisters, I plead with you to give your bodies to God because of all he has done for you. Let them be a living and holy sacrifice—the kind he will find acceptable. This is truly the way to worship him. Don't copy the behavior and customs of this world, but let God transform you into a new person by changing the way you think. Then you will learn to know God's will for you, which is good and pleasing and perfect.

Because of the privilege and authority God has given me, I give each of you this warning: Don't think you are better than you really are. Be honest in your evaluation of yourselves, measuring yourselves by the faith God has given us
    Romans 12: 1-3 (NLT)

    Faithfulness is a quality that God expects us to uphold to Him first, then to our family and friends. Being faithful is a quality that God holds in high esteem and expects us to operate and function in on a daily basis.

I have to admit that I have not been as faithful and loyal to God as I have been to my family, even though He has been beyond faithful to me.

Gentleness

*Put them in mind to be subject to principalities and
powers, to obey magistrates, to be ready to every good
work. To speak evil of no man, to be no brawlers,
but gentle, shewing all meekness unto all men.*
Titus 3:1-2

Being gentle is a fruit of the spirit that I have struggled with. God wants us to be gentle when dealing with people and situations. There comes a time in our lives when being too gentle opens the door for being hurt or misused. Always remember that there is a time to be gentle to some and a time for tough love. Keeping in mind that a gentle touch or word can lead someone to their deliverance and healing.

Self-Control
Listening and Doing

Understand this, my dear brothers and sisters: You must all be quick to listen, slow to speak, and slow to get angry. Human anger does not produce the righteousness God desires. So get rid of all the filth and evil in your lives, and humbly accept the word God has planted in your hearts, for it has the power to save your souls.
James 1: 19-20 (NLT)

Self-control, the last fruit of the spirit is the most difficult of them all because it has kept me in a constant battle between my spirit and my flesh. Knowing that my flesh has desired and craved immediate self-gratification by any means necessary.

This world that we live in has become more self-centered than God centered which causes us to want things that He has openly said "no" to.

We need self-control in our lives if we plan to have any hope in getting cleaned up and sanctified to the degree that God would like to get us to in this life.

Conclusion

During the summer months especially, I make sure that I treat myself to pedicures. I love it when the softness and smoothness is revealed once the dead skin had been stripped away from my feet. It is something how layer after layer of dead skin can be removed time and time again if you take the time to have a pedicure done. It's the same feeling that I have experienced when God stripped away and forgave me of the sins that I had committed. Even though I was hiding behind the scars and the brokenness, I can now see how worthy I really am.

It's also amazing what God can do through you when you are obedient. God has taken me to a place where I want to stay. I am so elated by the fact that I have allowed myself to follow the voice of the Lord. God had to strip me of a lot of things in order to get me to a place and point to hear Him and only Him. Beneath the scars and brokenness, He allowed me to see my worth. Writing *Even Me* has taught me that no matter how jacked up and filthy you are, God can still use you.

God gave me two specific instructions about who I was supposed to share this plan with. To start off, he gave me five people during the first phase, six people during the second, and seven at the end. Some of the people that I wanted to run and tell I couldn't. He said that if you told them, they would not be able to understand nor handle it. I could not wait to share the news with them.

I knew that I could trust these people if my life depended on it and God knew that He could trust them with His plan for my life. When I think about the role these people play in my life; they were able to give me exactly what I need to make this book come full circle. The map, the scripture, the prayers, the pusher, the messenger, the realist and the Women of Essence.

The Map

The first person I shared God's plan with was the one who had given me Joel Osteen's book to read. He provided me with the map for the task that I was given. When the book was shared with me, I had been dealing with a lot of stress and depression. I started reading the book on day six because of what I was dealing with. Once the month was over I started at the beginning of the next month. Day one of the book, "Think The Way God Thinks" No man has ever seen, heard or even imagine the wonderful things God has in store for those who love the Lord (1 Corinthians 2:9). It went on to say, "Think increase….think big…think expansive! That was the confirmation for what he had instructed me to do the day prior. I had to ask, Lord EVEN ME? Yes, even you.

The Scripture

On day two Joel Osteen's thought for that day was "Develop a Vision for Victory" "Behold I am doing a new thing, Can you not perceive it? (Isaiah 43:19). As I began to read a little further I came across Jeremiah 29:11, "My plans for you are good and not evil, to give you a future and a hope." Interesting I thought, because the second person on my shared list told me on day 1 to read Jeremiah 29:10-11 when I told her what God had instructed me to do. She was thrilled to hear about the good works that God was doing in my life.

The Prayers

The third person on the list has been praying for me since day one. You know seasoned saints would tell you what remedies to use for bumps and bruises, like Tussin, vinegar, and Epson salt. Her remedies were always to tell God and pray about it. Once I shared the information with her the tears that she shed described how happy she was for what God had chosen to do in my life.

By this time, I was on cloud nine and it was hard for me to explain what was going on. I played "Your Will" and "Even Me", so that she could understand where I was coming from. Again, her tears told the story and her prayers never stopped.

The Pusher

The fourth component is a couple: separate but combined as one. The first but fourth person that's on the list is one who will push and support me in whatever I want to do. If I told her that I was opening a peanut shack, she would be willing to work in it. If I told her that I wanted to become a sea shell collector and had to go waist deep in the ocean, she would walk with me even though we can't swim. If I told her that I had been seeking God and waiting for an answer, she would wait with me. She is not one to discourage or judge you, but she will push you until you reach your goal.

I recall one Christmas she gave me a claddagh charm for my charm bracelet. The charm had two hands with a heart in the middle. Her exact words to me were "these are my hands around your heart." God allowed me to give her my heart by sharing my hopes, dreams and desires and I am thankful that I can count on her to guard it.

The Messenger

It's funny how people can reveal things to you and you laugh at them. Well, that's what I did when I was told that I was going to write a book. I never thought I had the time to do something like that. I went to school for everything besides English and Journalism and never thought that I was skilled to do anything of the sort. It has been said by some that God will in fact give you the tongue of the learned and you won't have to go to school for it. This person spoke what God fixed in his mouth to say and God brought it to pass.

The Supporter

After consulting God about my life and decisions that I need to make, "the supporter" is the next person in line that I shared my ideas and decisions with. Regardless of the decision or the outcome, he always supports me till the end.

He has no reservation about speaking his mind and telling it like it is; even about the things that I don't want to hear nor face. If I find myself in tough situations, he will advise me accordingly. He is someone that I can always confide in and depend on.

Women of Essence

These women have really been instrumental throughout this journey. I have been linked to some amazing women who can and will talk the talk and walk the walk. Their role has exposed them to some hidden God-given talents that they didn't know existed inside of them. I have had the pleasure of knowing the Entertainer, the Entrepreneur, the Editor, the Encourager and the Educator. They have kept me lifted in more ways than they will ever know and I am so grateful for the instrumental roles that they have played in my life.

Remembering Where I Come From

Mommy

Charm is deceptive, and beauty does not last; but a woman who fears the LORD will be greatly praised. Reward her for all she has done. Let her deeds publicly declare her praise
Proverbs 31:30-31 (NLT)

My mother Patricia Byrd-Sturdivant has been the prime example of what a woman of substance looks like. I give you the uttermost respect for molding Nadia, Chas and myself into the women that we are. I thank you for not only living a wholesome and clean life before us; but for providing for us while being a single mother and grandmother.

I give you the highest respect for never allowing yourself to speak unkind words about my father and for never complaining about the things that you wanted to do for us; but was unable to.

I am proud to call you my mom-daddy and I thank God for the virtuous woman that we have to look up to.

Special Women:

I am so grateful to be connected to such wonderful women who I could always count on to feed me, give me a ride, educate and support me. Throughout my life beginning at middle school 'til now have been connected to some women who have and still treat me as if I am their own. Carolyn Blackwell "Cool Breeze", Barbara Jones, Brenda Wilkerson, Wynola Hawkins, Henrietta Robinson, Kay Wilson and Clarissa Wilkerson. Thank you for being there for me, you will always be in my heart.

My Best friend: Teauana

Teauana, thanks for being that shoulder to lean on, a pillow to cry on and a true friend to depend on. I am blessed to have such a wonderful friend like you to share "single parent "stories with. Our journey as "single parent best friends" is one that I wouldn't trade for the world. We are two amazing women, raising three amazing children.

Birthday Parties: $200
Dinner date with the kids: $60
Best Friends: "priceless"

My Inner Circle

I am grateful to have such wonderful people in my life who I can honestly call my true, supportive, never judging me but always encouraging me friends. Whenever I need you, you are always there: Barry Anderson, Henry Ash, Jr. Sheneque Brawley-Duncan, Sylvester Gillespie, Ivy Ellis, Lorna Kelly, Aprilia Hubbard-Kuhn, Camille Mackey, Nadia Y. Mitchell, John Nesbitt, Keisha Perry, Christan Poston, Adrienne Witherspoon and Jerry Smith.

Alisha Byrd

In Honor Of

I consider myself the luckiest person in the world because I have been blessed with the best grandparents that God created. Minnie and Jessie Byrd, the sugar and cream in my coffee. The sun that rises and set each day. They inspire me, encourage me, discipline me when I am wrong, and praise me when I have done right.

My grandparents raised me, put me through college, and encouraged me along the way. I will forever be grateful for all of their hard work, dedication and loyalty to our family.

Minnie and Jessie have been married for 66 years. They are the proud parents of 14 children; 9 girls: Nancy Smith,

Marilyn "Ann" Wallace, Katie Crockett, Chris Vinson, Pat "mommy", Kathy "Obby" Kelly, Mary "Mae" Sturdivant, Gail Barber and Angela Whisonant and 5 boys: Jessie Byrd, Jr., Ernest Byrd, Sammy Byrd, Anthony Byrd, and Ronnie Byrd who are all living.

They are the esteemed grandparents of 40 grand children, 41 great-grandchildren and 4 great-great grandchildren and a poodle "Charlie".

In Memory Of
Clay Anthony Sturdivant

John Young

Minnie Crosby Young

John "JD" Wallace

Monica Nicole Watson

Special Thank You

Rev. R. Thomas Wyatt and first lady Minister Tina Wyatt. I am beyond blessed to be under such wonderful leadership. Thank you for encouraging me on numerous occasions, when I wanted to give up and throw in the towel. Your ability to hear from the Lord and bless your people with the most illustrative sermons are heartfelt and treasured. I pray that God's anointing will forever be upon you.

Custom Photo
Jeff Hicks, Owner
Salisbury, NC
www.jeffhicks.photoreflect.com

Twanna Hopkins
Majesty Hair Salon
Spencer, NC

Since God chose you to be the holy people he loves, you must clothe yourselves with tenderhearted mercy, kindness, humility, gentleness, and patience. Make allowance for each other's faults, and forgive anyone who offends you. Remember, the Lord forgave you, so you must forgive others. Above all, clothe yourselves with love, which binds us all together in perfect harmony. And let the peace that comes from Christ rule in your hearts. For as members of one body you are called to live in peace. And always be thankful.

Colossians 3:12-15 (NLV)

CPSIA information can be obtained
at www.ICGtesting.com
Printed in the USA
BVHW042355180522
637357BV00003B/104/J